Original title:
Violet Droplets Beneath the Griffin Lathe

Copyright © 2025 Swan Charm
All rights reserved.

Author: Liina Liblikas
ISBN HARDBACK: 978-1-80562-012-9
ISBN PAPERBACK: 978-1-80563-533-8

Threads of Radiance in the Crafting Silence

In silence deep, the whispers weave,
A tapestry of dreams, believe.
Golden threads in twilight spun,
Creating worlds where shadows run.

Beneath the moon's soft silken glow,
Faint echoes of the heart's true flow.
Each stitch a secret, softly sown,
In the quiet, seeds are grown.

With needles sharp, intentions clear,
Crafted with hope, dispelled all fear.
In the stillness, magic hums,
A gentle pulse, creation comes.

Amidst the calm, a flicker bright,
Tiny sparks ignite the night.
From crafting silence, beauty sings,
Unlocking all that dreaming brings.

So let us tread this tranquil path,
Where artisans of light will laugh.
In every corner, every seam,
Threads of radiance softly gleam.

Constellations Woven in Ethereal Colors

In realms where starlight bends and plays,
Colors dance in cosmic ways.
Nebulas in hues divine,
Whispers of the grand design.

Gossamer threads in the twilight spun,
Map the journeys never done.
Each hue a tale, a wish to chart,
A universe painted from the heart.

As comets tail with fiery grace,
Woven dreams in an endless space.
In night's embrace, the colors swirl,
Constellations' secrets unfurl.

Echoes of old, in silver bright,
Guide the wanderer through the night.
With every step, the colors sing,
A tapestry that fate shall bring.

So gaze upon the heavens wide,
In every twinkle, worlds abide.
For in this vast, enchanting show,
Ethereal colors softly glow.

Alchemical Ballet of Light and Shadow

In chambers deep where sorcery reigned,
Light and shadow, endlessly strained.
Golden rays in a silken sweep,
Dancing softly, secrets to keep.

The alchemists' whispers mix and flow,
Turning base into gold with a glow.
In every twirl and every leap,
The dance of fate begins to creep.

Through crystal jars and flasks aglow,
Potent visions begin to grow.
With every movement, a spell in flight,
Crafting magic of day and night.

As shadows swirl, they intertwine,
Breath of darkness, essence divine.
In the ballet of the light's embrace,
We find the heart of time and space.

So let us twirl in this mystic game,
The dance of life, love's ancient flame.
In the alchemical blend we find,
The harmony of heart and mind.

The Whirlwind of Celestial Inspirations

In the tempest where thoughts collide,
Celestial wonders will not hide.
Ideas swirl like leaves in gales,
Inspiration flows, and never fails.

With every breath, the cosmos calls,
A symphony of light that enthralls.
Through swirling stardust, dreams take flight,
A whirlwind crafting day from night.

The ether hums with whispers sweet,
Bestowing visions at our feet.
In each turn, a spark ignites,
A dance of destiny ignites.

From every corner of the sky,
Echoes linger, thoughts that fly.
In every flicker, heartbeats rise,
Most splendid truths in hidden skies.

So let us brave this cosmic storm,
Where dreams take shape, and spirits warm.
In the whirlwind, find the spark,
Celestial inspirations light the dark.

Transformations in the Luminous Workshop

In a room where shadows gleam,
Hands weave magic with a dream.
Brass and silver come alive,
In the glow, the spirits thrive.

Glisten of the tools at play,
Each creation finds its way.
Whispers float on candlelight,
As night dances with delight.

From fire's kiss, the forms arise,
Chasing warmth, they touch the skies.
Artistry in every beat,
Crafted hearts and minds compete.

Each frame holds a tale untold,
With mysteries in every fold.
Craftsmen sing in joyful tune,
Their spirits lifted, painted moon.

So in this place where dreams ignite,
Magic weaves both day and night.
Transformations softly dance,
In the luminous workshop's trance.

Shadows Singing in Ethereal Crafted Dreams

In the quiet, shadows blend,
Magic waits at every bend.
Songs of night, they softly rise,
Wrapped in mist beneath the skies.

Woven tales of hope and fear,
Echo softly, loud and clear.
Each breath stirs a haunting song,
Where the nightingale belongs.

Dreams that flutter, finding flight,
In the depths of velvet night.
Crafted in a whispered sound,
Lost in echoes all around.

A tapestry of light and shade,
Where forgotten wishes wade.
Shadows sing their melodies,
Carried on the evening breeze.

As the dawn begins to break,
All these visions softly wake.
In the light, a new design,
Breathing life to each entwined.

Celestial Currents of the Artisan's Heart

In the depths of silent space,
Artisans find their own grace.
Stardust flows through careful hands,
Crafting dreams like sea and sands.

Hammer strikes on metal pure,
Each creation strong and sure.
Celestial currents breathe and swell,
Tales of magic none can tell.

Galaxies of thought take form,
In each heart, a mighty storm.
Sparks of brilliance flash and gleam,
As the night unfolds its theme.

Workshops buzz with fervent zeal,
Crafting wonders that can heal.
Mending souls with every piece,
In the heart, the cosmos cease.

Every touch a wish bestowed,
Journeys shared along the road.
Where artisans create anew,
Celestial dreams brought into view.

The Breath of Stars in Metal's Embrace

In the cradle of the night,
Stars awaken, burning bright.
Their breath weaves through silver strands,
Guiding dreams with gentle hands.

Metal glimmers, soft and warm,
In its reach, all fears disarm.
Embraced by whispers from above,
Crafting tales of painted love.

Each creation sings of light,
Reflecting every starry sight.
In the dance of tools and time,
Dreams unfold, a subtle rhyme.

As the forge ignites the way,
Crafted wishes gently sway.
The breath of stars, a soft caress,
In metal's arms, we find our rest.

Stories etched in bronze and gold,
With every strike, a legacy told.
In the night's embrace, we dare,
To find our place among the rare.

Reflections of Essence in the Artisan's Touch

In quiet corners, shadows dance,
The artisan weaves a mystic trance.
With every stroke, a story spins,
A tapestry of dreams begins.

Each echo holds a whispered song,
Of ages past where spirits throng.
Her hands, a map of ancient lore,
Create a life forevermore.

Gold and silver, bright and rare,
Caught in moments, spun with care.
Crafted jewels of heart and soul,
In their gleam, the spirits roll.

Through sunlight's glow, reflections gleam,
In fluttering wings of a waking dream.
Her touch ignites the hidden fate,
Transforming whispers into state.

With every piece, a world unfurls,
A symphony of colors swirls.
In the artisan's hands, we find,
The echoes of our hearts entwined.

Timeless Beads in the Celestial Flow

From dusk till dawn, the beading starts,
With every thread, the cosmos imparts.
Timeless colors dance and weave,
In cosmic tapestries, we believe.

Each bead a star in the night sky,
A glimmer of dreams soars high.
Entwined in fate, they drift and play,
In celestial streams, they softly sway.

With gentle hands, the artisan seeks,
Harmony found in whispered peaks.
A journey traced on silent ground,
Where hidden spirits can be found.

In every curve, a story spins,
Connects us all with gentle grins.
The universe within our grasp,
In every bead, a tale to clasp.

Time flows on in vibrant hues,
A radiant dance of reds and blues.
With every thread, a bond we show,
As timeless beads in celestial flow.

The Language of the Hidden Smithy

In shadows deep, the smithy glows,
Where forged desires quietly flows.
Anvil echoes whisper fate,
Crafting wonders while we wait.

With each blow, a story told,
Of ancient secrets, brave and bold.
Sparks ignite in passion's kiss,
Transforming metals into bliss.

The forge's warmth, a breath of life,
In art, there lingers beauty's strife.
The language of the hidden not,
Resides in flames, where hope is wrought.

Hand and heart, a perfect blend,
Through time's embrace, the shapes extend.
In rushing embers, legends rise,
An artisan's truth beneath the skies.

In every bend, a dream unwinds,
In iron's heart, the spirit finds.
The hidden smithy, wise and vast,
Holds eternity in the steadfast.

Shivers of Color in the Artisan's Glow

In twilight's breath, colors collide,
With every hue, a journey rides.
Across the canvas, visions gleam,
An artisan's heart takes wing in dream.

Shivers of color, soft and bright,
Echo the whispers of the night.
Brush strokes dance, a fleeting sigh,
Painting secrets on the sky.

With palette rich, she sings her tune,
Capturing stars and the golden moon.
Every shade tells a tale anew,
In every blend, a world to view.

As daylight fades, her magic flows,
In vibrant waves, the spirit glows.
From shadowed corners, colors rise,
Transforming moments into skies.

Through colors bold and softly woven,
In the artisan's heart, dreams are chosen.
Shivers of color, bright and true,
Guide us all in life's debut.

Ethereal Hues Beneath the Artisan's Gaze

In twilight's warmth, colors play,
Brush strokes dance, whispers sway.
Canvas and heart blend as one,
Crafting stories under the sun.

A palette blooms, strange and bright,
Shadows flicker, dance with light.
Every hue, a tale untold,
In every fold, dreams unfold.

Textures woven from the air,
Crafted from the midnight fair.
Each detail sings, a soft decree,
Art speaks wonders, wild and free.

Beneath the artist's gentle hand,
Magic breathes on golden sand.
Visions drift like leaves in fall,
Echoing beauty, embracing all.

So here, where hues forever flow,
Time stands still, the heart will know.
In ethereal light, we find our place,
Lost within the artisan's grace.

Kaleidoscope of the Mystic Indents

In the mirror's depths, colors swirl,
A world unbound begins to unfurl.
Shapes and patterns twist and glide,
In the heart of dreams, where secrets hide.

Each fragment gleams, a story spun,
Dancing light in the realm of fun.
Capturing whispers of fate's design,
In every twist, a heartbeat's line.

Fleeting glimpses of shades divine,
A dance of moments, yours and mine.
Fractals born from the ink of night,
Shaping hopes, igniting light.

Through glassy realms, we drift and sway,
Chasing visions that lead astray.
In the kaleidoscope's embrace, we shiver,
Beneath its magic, we will quiver.

So let us wander, hand in hand,
In stunning hues, together we stand.
In every twist, our souls align,
Boundless joy in each design.

Fragments of Lavender in the Night

Beneath the stars, lavender lies,
A soothing scent, where stillness sighs.
Whispers of dusk, a gentle breeze,
Carrying calm through the swaying trees.

Moonlight drapes on petals bright,
Casting silvers in the quiet night.
Each bloom a secret, softly kept,
In nature's cradle, dreams are crept.

Shadows dance in lavender's hold,
Stories of magic quietly told.
Underneath the vast, dark sky,
Fragments of peace begin to fly.

The nightingale sings, a sweet retreat,
Echoing softly, a rhythmic beat.
While lavender sways, lost in trance,
Inviting the world to join the dance.

So linger here, let worries part,
In this garden, we'll find our heart.
With each soft breath, the light ignites,
In fragments of lavender, our joys take flight.

Glistening Tears of the Lost Artisan

In shadows deep, the artisan weeps,
For dreams once bright, now silence keeps.
Glistening tears like rain on stone,
Echo lost visions the heart had known.

Chisels chip away at despair,
Fragments fly, a poignant air.
Each teardrop holds an untold tale,
Of passion's fight, of hope's frail veil.

With trembling hands, the soul revives,
In broken pieces, the artist thrives.
Crafted moments from sorrow's hand,
Carved in beauty, forever should stand.

In dim-lit rooms where shadows dwell,
The lost tools whisper, stories swell.
Each tear a token of love's sweet ache,
In every sorrow, new paths we make.

So gather the tears, let them shine,
For in each drop lies art divine.
The lost artisan finds strength anew,
In glistening tears, dreams born from blue.

Voices of the Night in Sculpted Essence

In the glow of twilight's grace,
Shadows dance in soft embrace.
Whispers weave through ancient trees,
Lending life to midnight's breeze.

Crickets sing a lullaby,
Stars awake, the dreams descend.
Every leaf in silence sighs,
Where the dusk and starlight blend.

Moonlight drapes the world in white,
Illuminating hidden trails.
Each soft rustle, a secret's flight,
In the heart where magic sails.

Wandering spirits softly tread,
Footsteps lost on woven air.
In the dreamscape, fears are shed,
As the night reveals its care.

Voices call from far and near,
Echoes carved in curves of night.
In this realm, the heart draws near,
Finding peace in silver light.

Glistening Pathways in a Dreamlike Haven

Footsteps trace the misty dawn,
Where enchantments softly call.
Petals glisten, dreams are drawn,
In this haven, spells enthrall.

Rivers of light like diamonds flow,
Winding through a tranquil glade.
Every shimmer a tale we know,
In the warmth of sun's cascade.

Echoes of laughter fill the air,
With each heartbeat, we create.
Nature's canvas, bold and fair,
In this moment, lives await.

Among the trees, a gentle sigh,
Whispers shared in sacred peace.
As shadows dance, the spirits fly,
In this realm, our troubles cease.

Beneath the arch of azure skies,
We weave our dreams in silver seams.
All our worries drift and rise,
Lost within these peaceful beams.

Harmonies of Radiant Whisperings

In a garden of twilight hues,
Songs of starlight gently play.
Every note, a moment's muse,
Carrying the night away.

Voices blend in sweet refrain,
Nature's choir, pure and bright.
Through the shadows soft as rain,
Woven dreams take graceful flight.

Birds in branches softly sing,
Melodies of evening's grace.
Every chime a gentle wing,
Floatings shadows, silent space.

Underneath the velvet sky,
Harmony dances in the breeze.
Lost in serenades, we fly,
Finding hope in nature's keys.

With each whisper, hearts align,
Echoes shared, a warming light.
In this world where souls entwine,
Dreaming deep into the night.

The Song of Craft Under Cosmic Gaze

In the forge of twilight's breath,
Crafting destinies with care.
Stars above, they whisper death;
Yet in shadows, dreams still dare.

Hammers strike, a rhythm true,
Echoes rise beneath the moon.
Pieces born of magic's hue,
Underneath the cosmic tune.

Each creation bound with fate,
Woven tales in iron cast.
With each stroke, the stars await,
Stories from the days long past.

In this dance of flame and steel,
Visions spark, ignite the night.
Crafting worlds where dreams reveal,
Every shadow holds the light.

Beneath the gaze of cosmic lore,
We bind our hopes in silent trust.
These creations, forevermore,
Will shine bright in stardust's dust.

Murmurs of the Mystical Lathe

In shadowed halls where whispers dwell,
Crafting dreams and tales to tell.
A dance of hands, a turn of wood,
Awakens magic, richly good.

The lathe spins secrets, old yet new,
With every curve, a life imbued.
From timber's heart, a shape takes flight,
Boundless visions, art's delight.

The shavings fall like autumn's leaf,
A sigh of beauty, a breath of grief.
In every grain, a story lies,
Of laughter, love, and countless sighs.

Glimmers in the dim-lit room,
Shape and shadow dance in bloom.
Voices gentle, echoes play,
As wood and magic weave away.

Together meld the craft and soul,
Embracing passion, making whole.
The lathe, a bridge from thought to form,
In its embrace, creation's warm.

Celestial Waters on the Edge of Creation

Where starlit skies meet tranquil shore,
The waves whisper secrets, a timeless lore.
Fluid magic, a cosmic stream,
Reflects our hopes, a dreamer's dream.

Each drop a wish that dances bright,
In silken tides, embracing night.
A ripple speaks of worlds afar,
A bridge of light, a shining star.

From depths unknown, the siren calls,
In whispered tones, through moonlit halls.
Elemental forces twirl and sway,
Holding tight the dreams we lay.

In currents wild, our spirits glide,
Amongst the stars, our fears subside.
Salty breeze, the heart's refrain,
Elysian shores, where love's not vain.

In shimmering tides, creation begins,
Celestial waters wash away sins.
And here we find, in liquid grace,
The universe, our sacred space.

The Healer's Artistry of Form

In quiet nooks where time stands still,
A healer weaves with gentle skill.
With eyes that see beyond the skin,
They mend the wounds that lie within.

Hands moving softly, a tender touch,
Reshaping lives, they care so much.
Through artful skill and ancient lore,
They guide the spirit to explore.

Potions brewed from nature's grace,
In every drop, a warm embrace.
A symphony of herbs and stone,
Together weaving flesh and bone.

In every pulse, a story speaks,
Of hidden battles, triumphs weak.
Through art and heart, the healer's song,
Transforms the weak, makes them strong.

With every breath, the healing flows,
A quiet power that lovingly grows.
In the sacred space, we find our way,
The healer's artistry, night and day.

Iridescent Traces of Forgotten Craft

In twilight's glow, where shadows meet,
A tale unfolds, bittersweet.
Crafts of old, by hands once skilled,
In whispers echo, dreams fulfilled.

Fine threads of color, woven wide,
Tell of moments we can't hide.
Patterns etched in time's embrace,
Iridescent memories in their place.

From clay to thread, the journey long,
Each craft, a verse of ancient song.
With every stitch, a wish is bound,
In every detail, life is found.

Forgotten hands once held the light,
Creating beauty in the night.
Those traces shine, a timeless art,
Awakening the world, heart to heart.

In every corner, stories gleam,
A tapestry, a vibrant dream.
Embracing forms, both lost and found,
In iridescent traces, joy resounds.

Ethereal Essence of the Crafting Light

In the glow of twilight's brush,
Dreams fracture in the loom of fate.
Threads of wisdom interweave,
Whispering secrets, old and great.

Fingers dance on shifting air,
Molding thought to form and grace.
Colors blend in careful hearts,
As shadows twist in warm embrace.

Spark of magic lingers near,
Softly touching all we see.
The essence bright, a radiant sphere,
Crafting light to set us free.

Souls connect through every stitch,
Woven tales that time can share.
In the quiet, dreams bewitch,
Singing songs of what we dare.

Where stars align in perfect rhyme,
Each creation starts to sing.
In the silence, whispers chime,
Crafting joy in everything.

Glistening Echoes in the Workshop's Heart

In the shadows, tools convey,
Stories clatter, sparks ignite.
Glistening echoes of the day,
Echo through the warm twilight.

Each hammer's strike, a rhythmic tune,
Resonating deep within.
The essence of the craft's cocoon,
Where dreams are born and lives begin.

Chisels carve in wood and stone,
Creating beauty from the bare.
In each grain, a tale is sewn,
Glistening echoes fill the air.

With each breath, the craftsman sighs,
The workshop hums a gentle song.
Whispers dance like fireflies,
Guiding hands that now belong.

As night descends, the shadows play,
In every nook, a soft delight.
Glistening dreams of yesterday,
Echo still, a lasting light.

The Alchemist's Veil of Purity

Beneath the stars, a quiet room,
Where potions brew and visions soar.
The alchemist treads through the gloom,
In search of truth forevermore.

In vessels clear, the colors dance,
Alchemy's secrets slowly blend.
Crafted fate holds a fleeting chance,
Whispers of what the heart can send.

A flick of wrist, a pinch of grace,
Transformations weave in whispered tones.
The veil of purity defines this space,
Where dreams evolve from countless stones.

Every drop a lesson learned,
In essence clear, the soul reflects.
The alchemist's fire, forever burned,
Guides them through life's many effects.

As twilight fades and shadows cast,
A tincture born of hope and peace.
The alchemist's dreams, a bond so vast,
In purity, their hearts release.

Dawn's Kiss on the Forged Metal

Kissed by dawn in golden rays,
The anvil glows with tender light.
Forged by hands in ancient ways,
Metal forms in morning bright.

Each strike resounds, a heartfelt song,
The rhythm echoes strength anew.
In artistry where dreams belong,
Dawn awakens every hue.

The forge ignites with fervent heat,
Breath of life in every arc.
Molten dreams, they swirl and meet,
In artistry, they leave their mark.

Transformed by flame, the metal sings,
A dance of sparks, a journey's start.
In the forge, a tale that clings,
Dawn's kiss ignites the crafting heart.

With every curve, a story told,
Of battles fought and glories won.
In strengthened steel, the brave and bold,
Find solace in the rising sun.

Echoes of the Astral Blueprints

In the hush of night's embrace,
Stars weave tales in silver trace.
Whispers swirl through cosmic seas,
Binding fate with gentle ease.

Colors dance on twilight's loom,
Mapping dreams where shadows bloom.
Galaxies spin in soft delight,
Echoes sing of endless flight.

From stardust's kiss, our paths arise,
Mirrored in the moonlit skies.
A tapestry of time and space,
Knitted closely, face to face.

In the depths of azure night,
We chart our course with endless sight.
Through portals vast and shimmering,
The heart of cosmos glimmering.

Each blueprint forged in ancient fire,
Holding secrets of desire.
With every pulse, we find our way,
In echoes where the shadows play.

The Weaver's Dreamscape of Enchantment

In a realm where dreams take flight,
Weavers spin with pure delight.
Threads of magic, soft and bright,
Dancing under the moon's soft light.

With every stitch, the visions flow,
Wondrous tales that ebb and glow.
Colors blend in twilight's hum,
In a world where wonders come.

Through whispered winds, the looms ignite,
Crafting wishes out of sight.
In the quiet, spells entwine,
Creating paths, both yours and mine.

In the heart of this enchanted space,
Harmony finds its rightful place.
With every note, the shadows sway,
In this dreamscape, night and day.

So close your eyes, let visions soar,
The weaver's magic evermore.
In the twilight, tales unfurl,
Whispers soft, a wondrous world.

Metaphysical Patterns in Cosmic Play

In the cosmos' gentle hand,
Patterns weave across the land.
Shapes of starlight, bold and true,
Echo dreams in shades of blue.

Through the currents of the night,
Wisps of wisdom guide the light.
Harmony of dark and bright,
Unfolding secrets, taking flight.

Each star a nod to what we seek,
Languages of the mystic speak.
Timeless echoes, bold and grand,
Craft a dance where truths expand.

In the chaos, find your peace,
As the universe grants release.
Patterns twist in cosmic sway,
Metaphysics in grand ballet.

Awakening in twilight's glow,
Nature's song begins to flow.
With every heartbeat, life's display,
We become part of cosmic play.

The Artisan's Symphony of Light

With brush and ink, the artisan starts,
Creating worlds with vibrant hearts.
Each stroke sings a new refrain,
A symphony in colors' gain.

Echoes of light in every hue,
Crafting visions, bold and true.
Dancing shadows, twirling bright,
Illuminating the depths of night.

In the silence, music sways,
Filling space in wondrous ways.
Notes like petals gently fall,
Filling the canvas, beckoning all.

As daylight blends with evening's grace,
Art unfolds in time and space.
Light and sound in harmony sing,
Crafting joy that dreams can bring.

So let your spirit take its flight,
Join the dance in shades of light.
For in this space, we find our might,
As artisans of pure delight.

Enigmatic Tears of the Celestial Beast

In the night where silence breathes,
A creature stirs beneath the eaves.
Its tears like stars, they fall and shine,
Each drop a wish, a tale divine.

With fur of night and eyes of gold,
It carries secrets, dreams untold.
Through misty woods, it roams the skies,
Guarding the realm where magic lies.

Once whispered near a willow's weep,
Its heart in shadows, buried deep.
For those who seek and dare to find,
A thread of fate entwined in mind.

The moon shall guide, the stars shall weave,
A path where few dare to believe.
A symphony of light and gloom,
Within the depths of twilight's bloom.

With each soft sigh, the night awakes,
A tapestry of dreams it makes.
Embrace the tears from skies above,
For in their glow, we find our love.

Shadows of Amethyst in the Twilight

When twilight paints the sky in hues,
With whispers soft, the shadows muse.
Amethyst gems adorn the night,
Casting spells of wondrous light.

In every glint, a story weaves,
Of ancient woods where magic breathes.
Dreamers tread on paths of lore,
In search of dreams, forever more.

The air is thick with secrets kept,
Where moonlit guardians have wept.
They watch the dance of fading day,
As twilight beckons dreams to stay.

With every star, a wish alights,
In shadows deep, where magic bites.
Flickers of fate in soft embrace,
Capturing time, a fleeting trace.

In amethyst dusk, we dwell,
Where echoes of enchantments swell.
Beneath the veil of night's caress,
We find our truths, our hearts confess.

Whispers of Lavender from the Artisan's Hand

In gardens where the lavender blooms,
An artisan spins magic looms.
With gentle hands that craft the air,
Each whisper holds a tale so rare.

The scent of dreams in twilight's glow,
With petals soft, the spirit flows.
From brush to clay, creations rise,
As colors dance beneath the skies.

With every stitch, a story's told,
Of love and laughter, memories bold.
In every thread, a journey sown,
Within the heart, a seed has grown.

Amongst the hues of purple night,
Awake the dreams, embrace the light.
For artisans with souls of grace,
Leave traces of their sacred space.

In whispers soft, the lavender sings,
A melody of timeless things.
Awake the world, let magic flow,
For in this craft, the heart will glow.

Chimeric Reflections from the Workshop

In the workshop where wonders dwell,
Chimeric tales weave their spell.
Between the tools and dusty air,
Creativity blooms with tender care.

With pieces rare and moments bright,
Each crafted form, a dream takes flight.
From wood and stone, to fabric fine,
Creation flows, a dance divine.

A sculptor's hand, a painter's sigh,
They breathe life into dreams that fly.
Each artifact, a world apart,
Reflects the whispers of the heart.

In shadows cast by lantern's glow,
The stories of the chimeras grow.
With every spark and every roar,
The workshop holds a magic core.

Unraveled threads of time await,
To shape the fate that lies in fate.
A chimeric dance of dusk and dawn,
In every piece, a dream reborn.

Shimmering Secrets of the Hidden Smith

In a forge where shadows dance,
The echoes of the hammers glance,
Secrets whispered, wrought in fire,
Crafted dreams that lift us higher.

Beneath the anvil's ancient moan,
A tale of metal, finely honed,
With every stroke, a story spun,
Of legends lost, and battles won.

The sparks ignite in twilight's grip,
As molten stars in darkness slip,
Each gleam a promise, each flash a wish,
In the heart of a smith, where magic is rich.

Hidden chambers, timeless space,
Where every tool finds its own place,
With every creation, a soul reborn,
From the ashes of yore, a new dawn's worn.

So by the fire, secrets gleam bright,
A smith's soft whispers to the night,
In shimmering shadows, we find our path,
For the art of creation holds nature's wrath.

Wistful Weavings of a Celestial Dream

In twilight's embrace, the stars align,
We weave through realms, through space and time,
Wistful whispers on the night air flow,
Hopes and wishes in a gentle glow.

Threads of silver, soft and light,
Knit together in the velvet night,
Dreams take shape with a tender grace,
In this realm, we find our place.

The moon, a loom of gossamer beams,
Crafting solace from our fleeting dreams,
As constellations guide our flight,
We dance among the stars so bright.

Through portals of thought, we softly drift,
With every memory, our spirits lift,
In moments where the heartstrings bind,
We stitch the fabric of the mind.

So let us wander, hand in hand,
Through the wonder of a dreamy land,
For in our weavings, truth unfolds,
In wistful echoes, a tale retold.

The Chisel's Call in a Mystic Realm

In a realm where shadows speak,
The chisel's song begins to leak,
Into the stone, a whisper flows,
Revealing secrets, the heart bestows.

With every tap, a form emerges,
From rugged depths, the spirit surges,
A dance of art, where hands align,
Chiseling fate from the divine.

Inscribe the stories left untold,
A journey woven, brave and bold,
The mystic realm, a sacred space,
Where time is paused in soft embrace.

Crafted visions, dark and light,
Every stroke ignites the night,
The chisel's call, a haunting tune,
Echoing 'neath the silver moon.

So let the stone sing out its name,
For every piece holds glory and flame,
In the chisel's art, we find the way,
To shape the dreams of yesterday.

Phantasmal Reflections on the Inkwell's Surface

In the inkwell's depths, shadows blend,
Phantasmal whispers, stories lend,
With every drop, the ink takes flight,
Revealing tales hidden from sight.

Fingers dance with a quill in hand,
As visions rise from the soft, damp sand,
Reflections mirror in the liquid dark,
Illuminating dreams, sparking a spark.

Each swirl a pathway, each line a note,
In the symphony of thoughts we wrote,
Voices echo in the ink's embrace,
A canvas alive, a sacred space.

Through the murmur of the quill's swift trace,
We capture moments, a fleeting grace,
Phantoms linger on the page anew,
In every story, a world to view.

So dip your soul in the inkwell's hue,
Let reflections guide what's truest to you,
For in this realm of script and sign,
Phantasms dwell, both yours and mine.

The Radiance Hidden Within

In shadows deep, a spark awaits,
A whisper caught in silence fates.
Within the heart, a glow will rise,
Unveiling dreams beneath the skies.

A gentle flicker, soft yet bright,
Defying darkness, claiming light.
Beneath the surface, gold does gleam,
Awakening the hidden dream.

With every breath, a promise swells,
Of magic held in secret spells.
A journey waits, both wild and tame,
To trace the pulse of one's true name.

Through tangled paths where spirits roam,
The soul finds solace, finds its home.
Embrace the light, let shadows part,
For radiance blooms within the heart.

As dawn breaks forth, a canvas clear,
Each stroke declares, "The time is near!"
So forge ahead, through dark and dim,
And let your light dance free and trim.

Subtle Currents of Creation's Touch

In hidden streams where magic flows,
Creation hums, and wisdom grows.
A gentle hand shapes clay and stone,
Crafting worlds with echoes known.

As whispered winds through branches weave,
A tapestry of dreams conceive.
Each thread a tale, a life entwined,
Bound by the art of heart and mind.

In quietude, a spark ignites,
Illuminating starry nights.
Where visions dance and shadows play,
The soul finds peace in making sway.

With every brush, with every pen,
The heart breathes life again and again.
The stillness sings, the colors sigh,
As stars awaken in the sky.

In every stroke, a spirit lingers,
Crafted with love by deftest fingers.
Subtle currents guide their flow,
In the realms where art will grow.

Imaginary Landscapes of the Artisan's Soul

In realms unseen, where dreams collide,
An artist's heart, a worlds' wide tide.
With every tale, a landscape blooms,
Where nothing fades, and all resumes.

Mountains rise from whispers soft,
And valleys cradle thoughts aloft.
With colors bright and shadows deep,
The artisan awakes from sleep.

Through meadows lush, where wonders sigh,
Broad strokes of love touch every sky.
The streams of ink, the winds of sound,
Carve pathways new, where hope is found.

Eternal echoes in the air,
Paint memories with utmost care.
Imagined sights, in hearts unfurled,
Craft worlds anew from round the world.

With every hand, a story's spun,
A universe where all is one.
In artistry, the truth can dwell,
As spirit breathes within the shell.

The Light Between Every Turn

In winding paths where shadows wane,
There lies a light, unmarred by pain.
Each step unveils, each turn reveals,
The gems of life that fate conceals.

A flicker bright in darkest night,
A beacon calling souls to flight.
Through tangled woods and winding streams,
The heart explores its whispered dreams.

With every breath, and every sigh,
A new adventure calls us high.
The light that dances, pure and true,
A compass set for me and you.

Embrace the journey, trust the way,
The light will guide through night and day.
In every corner, turn, and bend,
A radiance found, a path to mend.

So wander forth, let spirits soar,
In moments shared, we are much more.
The light between each turn we take,
A promise kept, a bond we make.

Beyond the Forge: Dreams in the Air

In shadows deep, the flames do dance,
Where dreams are born, and time may chance.
With hammer's strike and metal's song,
The echoes weave where hopes belong.

A whisper soft, the breezes call,
To carry dreams both big and small.
As stars align in cosmic play,
Their glimmers guide the lost astray.

Each ember glows with stories old,
Of wizards wise and hearts of gold.
Through swirling mist, the visions leap,
Awake the dreams long lost in sleep.

In twilight's grasp, the night draws near,
With silken threads that shimmer clear.
We journey forth, our spirits free,
Through realms unknown, for all to see.

So cast your gaze beyond the flame,
Embrace the fervor, feel the same.
For in the forge of dreams we find,
The hidden truths of humankind.

Cadence of the Twilight Smith

Beneath the stars where shadows weave,
The twilight smith begins to cleave.
With steady hands and focused gaze,
He shapes the night through artful ways.

The anvil rings in rhythmic beat,
As atmospheres in silence greet.
His hammer glints in twilight's glow,
With every strike, new worlds to sow.

Enchantments swirl in swirling air,
The scent of magic everywhere.
From molten fire and silver thread,
The dreams of night begin to spread.

In candlelight, the shadows dance,
As secrets drift in quiet chance.
The twilight whispers soft and low,
Revealing paths the heart may know.

So listen close, take heed of fate,
In cadence wrought, the night awaits.
For every forge creates anew,
A tapestry of skies so blue.

Illumination from the Bewitched Bellows

With bellows breathing life anew,
The flames ignite in spectral hue.
In chamber dim, where visions flare,
The artisans craft enchantment rare.

Through smoke and ash, the stories rise,
Reflections bright like morning skies.
Each spark a tale, each flicker thought,
From depths of craft, all wonders sought.

The rhythms dance in chorus bright,
As shadows meld with the glowing light.
With every breath, a secret shared,
In luminous arcs, the fates are dared.

So wield your tools with heart ablaze,
For magic lives in humble ways.
In every blow, a dream takes form,
From forged desire, a future born.

As twilight falls and whispers call,
Bewitched bellows rise, enthrall.
In shimmering warmth of glowing night,
The craftsman's art unveils the light.

Gem-Heart of the Celestial Craftsman

Deep in the realm where starlight gleams,
The craftsman weaves his wondrous dreams.
With gem-heart bright and skillful hand,
He shapes the cosmos, vast and grand.

Through crystal clear, the light refracts,
Each facet holds the world intact.
In gentle arcs, the colors blend,
Creating worlds that never end.

The fabric of the heavens hums,
With melodies where magic comes.
In every stone, a secret lies,
A universe behind the eyes.

So seek the gems that caught your gaze,
Each one infused with timeless praise.
For in their depths, a spark ignites,
A journey born on starry nights.

Embrace the craft, let spirits fly,
For in the heart, true wonders lie.
The celestial craftsman's work is clear,
In every gem, the stars draw near.

Emblems of Essence on the Turner's Table

Upon the table, wood does spin,
A dance of grain, where dreams begin.
Each gentle touch, a whisper's grace,
In every curve, a tale's embrace.

The chisel bites, the shavings fly,
By candlelight, the visions lie.
Emblems formed from heart's deep wood,
A legacy of thought, a brotherhood.

Shimmering dust, the artist's breath,
Crafting life, defying death.
With every twist, the essence learned,
A universe in silence turned.

The lathe hums soft, a calming sigh,
As shapes emerge, like dreams that fly.
In focused hands, the world stands still,
The art of life, a craftsman's will.

Time's gentle hand, it soon will fade,
Yet on this table, memories laid.
In wood and grain, a story told,
Through emblems of essence, bold.

Reflections of the Starlit Hands

Beneath the sky, where shadows dance,
Starlit hands weave chance and glance.
With fingers tracing paths of light,
The cosmos sings through deepest night.

Glimmers echo in velvet dark,
Wonders whisper, igniting spark.
The quiet heart of night unveils,
Legends born in twilight trails.

In every star, a dream takes flight,
Carved from whispers, pure delight.
Together they weave tales of old,
Each twinkle speaks, a truth retold.

Hands lifted high, the sky embraces,
A tapestry of night's vast spaces.
Reflections dance in midnight streams,
Where silence births the brightest dreams.

With starlit tears, the night does weep,
Harvesting secrets that shadows keep.
In cosmic rhythm, the visions play,
Reflections guide the dawn's new day.

The Spirit's Craft Beneath Shimmering Skies

Under skies where shadows blend,
The spirit's craft, where dreams ascend.
With every stroke, the canvas sighs,
Awakening worlds through painted skies.

Colors swirl in the gentle breeze,
Whispers echo among the trees.
In each hue, a story stirs,
Crafted echoes of life's soft murmurs.

The brush glides with a tender grace,
As if the air itself finds space.
Beneath the arch of twilight's glow,
The spirit whispers, soft and slow.

Stars above, they shimmer bright,
Guiding hands through the endless night.
In every line, a path unfolds,
The spirit's craft, a joy retold.

With vivid dreams, the canvas breathes,
In every stroke, the heart believes.
Beneath the skies, where stories lie,
The spirit's art shall never die.

In the Heart of a Celestial Workshop

In the heart, where stars do glow,
A workshop forged in cosmic flow.
With hammers raised and spirits bright,
They weave the whispers of the night.

Galaxies spin in wondrous haste,
Crafting dreams with celestial taste.
Each flick of the wrist, a comet's tail,
In this workshop, no heart can fail.

From stardust, wonders take their form,
A symphony of light, a swirling storm.
Every craft speaks of tales unknown,
In the heart, where seeds are sown.

With laughter ringing through time and space,
Creating joy in this timeless place.
Echoes of the past take flight,
In the heart of the workshop's light.

Through every toil, a purpose grows,
As cosmic streams, the spirit flows.
In the heart of those who dare to dream,
Here, life is more than what it seems.

Whispers of Amethyst Mist

In valleys deep where shadows play,
The mist of amethyst swirls and sways,
It carries secrets, soft and light,
Whispers of dreams in the cool of night.

Beneath the moon, a phantom's song,
Guides weary hearts where they belong,
Each note a promise, a gentle kiss,
In the tender glow of the twilight mist.

The trees stand tall, their branches weave,
Stories of lovers who dared believe,
With every sigh, the night reveals,
A world where magic and wonder heals.

Through fields of lavender, flowers bloom,
Bathed in mystique, dispelling gloom,
The air is laced with ethereal grace,
In amethyst whispers, we find our place.

So linger here, let time unwind,
In the heart of night, true peace you'll find,
For all the dreams that gently persist,
Are woven softly in amethyst mist.

Secrets of the Celestial Forge

In the heart of stars, the ancients tread,
With hammers of light, forging what's said,
They shape the dawn, the dusk's embrace,
In the celestial forge, a wondrous place.

Winds of creation whisper as they flow,
Bringing to life what night will sow,
Each flicker a tale, a promise bright,
Crafted by constellations' pure light.

With every strike, a new world begins,
Lost in a rhythm of cosmic spins,
The dance of elements, fierce and bold,
Crafts the universe, stories untold.

Galaxies form, like diamonds in the dark,
Blessings of hope in every spark,
The secrets entwined in fiery grace,
Reveal the magic of time and space.

So let us gaze at the skies above,
And ponder the stars with wonder and love,
For in their shining, the truth implores,
The endless journey from the forge's doors.

Twilight Tears of the Sphinx

In twilight's embrace, the sphinx does weep,
As shadows stretch and secrets seep,
Her tears like jewels on sands so fine,
Hold mysteries deep, lost in time.

She guards the dusk with a silent gaze,
Through endless nights and timeless days,
With riddles spun from the twilight air,
Inviting the brave to linger and dare.

Where dreams collide with reality's thread,
In her gaze lies the path to tread,
Each tear a tale, each sigh a clue,
In the twilight haze, the moment's true.

Held in her heart are shadows of fate,
Whispers of ages that patiently wait,
For those who seek to unveil the night,
In twilight's tears, find their heart's light.

So seek the sphinx when the sun does die,
Let her riddles carry you high,
For in her sorrow lies a world to see,
Where the twilight tears hold the key.

Enchanted Rain over Metal Wings

When rain cascades on metal wings,
A symphony of magic sings,
Each drop a note in the cool night air,
Enchanting all with its gentle flare.

The wings do glisten, polished bright,
Dancing shadows in the dim twilight,
As if alive with dreams unfurled,
Carrying whispers from another world.

Beneath the storm, the earth awakens,
Magic flows in the hearts of the taken,
Nature and metal in a lovers' dance,
Caught in the grip of a fleeting chance.

As thunder rolls, the sky ignites,
A ballet of colors in dazzling flights,
In the rain's embrace, the world seems new,
An enchantment felt by those who pursue.

So let your spirit take to the skies,
On metal wings where adventure lies,
For in the rain's fall, a promise rings,
Of endless journeys on enchanted wings.

Luminance of the Lavender Rain

In twilight's whisper, blooms unfold,
A lavender dream, its tales retold.
With every drop, enchantments weave,
A tapestry of night, we believe.

The moon dips low, in gentle grace,
Cocooned in scents, a soft embrace.
Each pearl of rain, a wish sent high,
To dance with stars in the velvet sky.

Shadows come alive, with flickers bright,
Beneath the clouds, a flickering light.
A lullaby sung by the breeze,
Our hearts alight, we find our ease.

Embers of dusk, in harmony sway,
As dreams awaken in the lavender spray.
A symphony born of the night's refrain,
In every petal, the magic remains.

So step with care in this twilight land,
Where lavender rain meets the whispering sand.
With every heartbeat, a world anew,
In luminance bright, we bloom like dew.

Echoes from the Iron Aviary

In shadows cast by wings of steel,
A world awakens, wild and real.
With iron songs that pierce the night,
The echoes of dreams take flight.

Beneath the arches, a whisper flows,
Where iron birds weave tales that glow.
They sing of journeys, far and wide,
With hearts ablaze, and souls as guides.

The clang of hope reverberates,
Through ancient walls, it reverberates.
Each note ascends, a gem refined,
In the iron aviary, peace we find.

Through swirls of smoke, the tales arise,
Of soaring dreams that touch the skies.
And every clang, a wish we'll send,
On iron wings, our hearts ascend.

So listen close to the echoes clear,
In the iron aviary, we shed our fear.
For in each note, a world awaits,
Where iron dreams unlock the gates.

Crystalline Blossoms in the Forge's Heart

Within the forge, where shadows dance,
Crystalline blooms take their chance.
From molten fires, they rise anew,
In vibrant hues, a spectrum grew.

The anvil sings with fervent light,
Casting dreams in the dead of night.
Each blossom formed, a tale to tell,
Of struggle, hope, of rise and fell.

In whispered tones, the metals sigh,
As petals gleam and spirits fly.
A harmony forged from sweat and tears,
In crystalline gardens, dispelling fears.

Their beauty shines in the darkest night,
A testament to relentless might.
Every heart beats with fire and grace,
In the forge's heart, we find our place.

So linger here, where dreams ignite,
In crystalline blossoms, the world feels right.
For in each glimmer, a spark we see,
In the forge's embrace, we're forever free.

Glistening Hues of the Mythic Tail

Beneath the moon's ethereal glow,
The mythic tail begins to flow.
In hues of wonder, stories spin,
A canvas bright, where dreams begin.

With every flick, a tale unfolds,
Of ancient realms and legends bold.
Together, we chase the fleeting light,
Through portals of twilight, taking flight.

A dance of colors, wild and free,
In shimmering waves, the world we see.
Each glistening hue, a wish so bright,
Painting the sky with pure delight.

In the depth of night, our spirits rise,
To grasp the stars, to claim the skies.
With every twinkle, a promise made,
In myth and magic, our hearts cascaded.

So follow close, where mysteries weave,
In glistening hues, we come to believe.
For in the mythic tail, we shall find,
The whispers of the universe aligned.

The Forgotten Elixirs of Celestial Craft

In hidden glades, the whispers call,
Elixirs lost, beneath the thrall.
Stars once bright, now dimmed and cold,
In vials crafted from stories old.

Moonlight drops in crystal streams,
Chasing shadows, chasing dreams.
With every drop, a secret keeps,
Awakened magic in the deep.

Potion brews with fire's dance,
A fleeting chance, a daring glance.
Yet in the heart, the truth does stir,
Celestial art, a timeless blur.

Through ages lost, their tales breathe life,
In the chaos, shines the strife.
Forgotten visions steep in night,
While starlit eyes behold the light.

Adventure awaits, for those who seek,
In whirling winds, the lost tongues speak.
Each elixir, a heartbeat's churn,
For curious souls who long to learn.

Lavender Soaked Serenade of the Faerie Forge

By gentle streams, where whispers sigh,
Lavender blooms reach for the sky.
In faerie forges, magic swells,
With each sweet note, a tale compels.

Sparks of twilight, dancing bright,
Filling the air with pure delight.
In petals soft, the secrets lay,
Of dreams that linger, day by day.

They sing of hearts, both brave and true,
Of endless skies and endless dew.
Lavender kissed by the morning's grace,
In faerie realms, a warm embrace.

The forge alights with colors bold,
A serenade of stories told.
In whispered tones, their laughter weaves,
A tapestry of what one believes.

So close your eyes, let visions soar,
In lavender dreams, there's always more.
As faeries dance beneath the trees,
Their songs entwine with evening breeze.

Shards of Twilight Woven in Metal

In twilight's grasp, where shadows blend,
Shards of dreams begin to mend.
Through iron hands, the magic flows,
In whispered vows the metal glows.

Cloaked in mist, where secrets hide,
Forged in fires where hope and pride.
Every strike, a heartbeat found,
As echoes linger all around.

Along the anvil, tales unfold,
In shimmering threads of silver and gold.
The night's embrace, a soothing balm,
In crafted works, a potent charm.

With every spark, the stories bloom,
Of ancient spells that light the gloom.
Shards collide beneath the stars,
Beneath the weight of ancient scars.

In twilight's dance, creation sings,
Of ferrous dreams and fragile wings.
So heed the call of forge and fire,
In every shard, a deep desire.

Dreams Forged in the Light of Dawn

As dawn awakes from slumber deep,
The whispered dreams begin to leap.
In morning's glow, the world ignites,
With threads of gold, the day invites.

Echoes of night begin to fade,
In every shadow, a promise laid.
Forged in light, the heart takes flight,
To chase the dreams that shine so bright.

Hope blooms wide in every ray,
As.colors dance, and shadows play.
With every breath, a chance to start,
In the dawn's warmth, a yearning heart.

So gather strength as morning breaks,
For every step the journey makes.
In dreams reborn, let worries cease,
In the light of dawn, we find our peace.

Embrace the day, let spirits soar,
In every moment, discover more.
For dreams are forged, as shadows wane,
In the light of dawn, we rise again.

The Cascade of Celestial Hues

In twilight's gentle grasp we find,
Colors swirling, intertwined.
A canvas painted by the night,
With stars that shimmer, soft and bright.

A dance of hues, a cosmic flow,
Whispers of secrets from below.
The moonlight bathes the world in grace,
Illuminating every space.

A river glows with silver tide,
Reflections of the dreams we hide.
Each ripple tells a tale anew,
A magic known to very few.

The sky, a tapestry of chance,
Calls us to join the cosmic dance.
In every turn, in every sigh,
A promise hidden in the sky.

So let us wander, hand in hand,
Through realms that none before have planned.
For in this cascade, we are free,
Boundless as the stars at sea.

Secrets of the Ethereal Grinders

In shadows deep where echoes weave,
Mysteries concealed, hard to perceive.
The grinders turn with silent glee,
Revealing what the heart must see.

Whirring wheels of stardust grind,
Shaping fate, both cruel and kind.
The whispers call from darkened vale,
Each secret spun, a timeless tale.

Ethereal glow in moonlit blaze,
A dance surrounded by a haze.
In every flicker, light will break,
Awakening dreams we thought would wake.

The bittersweet of time's embrace,
Crafts both sorrow and gentle grace.
In this realm of shifting time,
We find our rhythm, sweet as rhyme.

With every turn the world reclaims,
The threads of life, the shades of games.
In grinder's hands, our stories spin,
A tapestry where dreams begin.

Dreaming in Colors of the Elusive Forge

In darkness blooms a vibrant spark,
Colors form within the dark.
The forge ignites with whispers low,
Crafting dreams where visions flow.

Each shade distinct, yet all entwined,
Looming wonders, fate defined.
In swirls of light, we lose our way,
Chasing hues that softly sway.

The echoes rise, a symphony,
Of laughter stitched in harmony.
In every whisper, worlds collide,
In every heartbeat, dreams abide.

With molten hues like evening's glow,
The forge unveils what hearts can grow.
Each pulsating rhythm, pure delight,
In colors gleaming, vivid, bright.

Through the portal of the night,
We journey forth, past our own sight.
For in this forge, we come alive,
In colors bold, our spirits thrive.

Crystalline Whispers of Time's Embrace

In the stillness, time stands clear,
Crystalline whispers soothe our fear.
Each moment, precious, soft as snow,
A gentle truth we come to know.

Through fractured glass, the light cascades,
Reflecting dreams in fleeting shades.
A tapestry of moments lost,
Each memory, a tiny cost.

Time's gentle arms, a lover's hold,
Embracing stories yet untold.
The past is but a breath away,
In shattered shards, they find their play.

The echoes of the future call,
In whispers soft, we dance, we fall.
With every tick, a chance to glean,
The dance of fate, the unseen queen.

So linger here, where shadows blend,
In crystalline echoes, time will bend.
For in this space, we come to see,
The beauty of what's yet to be.

Echoes of the Unseen Artisan

In shadows deep, where whispers flow,
The artisan works, with magic aglow.
Hands that shape, and dreams that weave,
Silent echoes, in twilight's eve.

With every brush, a story spun,
The canvas hums, as creations run.
Mysteries rise, in colors bright,
Crafted wonders, in the night.

In gilded corners, secrets hide,
Each stroke a journey, a silent guide.
Through countless trials, the soul does mold,
An unseen hand, in the tales retold.

Resonance lingers, in every line,
Artisan's heart, a pulse divine.
A world reborn, with whispered grace,
In echoes soft, finds its place.

Among the stars, where dreams are sewn,
The unseen craftsman, never alone.
In the silence, their spirit gleams,
A tapestry woven from the seams.

Harmonies of the Crafting Night

Beneath the moon's soft silver glow,
Craftsmen gather, as shadows grow.
Tools in hand, with hearts attuned,
In crafting night, their dreams are pruned.

Each sound a note, in the cool air found,
Chisels sing, and hammers pound.
A symphony of wood and stone,
In whispered songs, their talents hone.

As lanterns flicker, and spirits thrive,
In the cradle of night, their hopes arrive.
Brushes dance, and colors blend,
With every strike, the magic mends.

Threads of fate are gently spun,
In the silence, all work is done.
Harmony flows, as shadows play,
The crafting night slips softly away.

So raise a glass to the artists' might,
Who weave their dreams in the heart of night.
For in each hand, a story's thread,
In harmonies sung, their visions spread.

The Dance of Glistening Sparks

In the forge where embers leap,
Glistening sparks in shadows creep.
A dance begins, with flames as light,
Artisans twirl, through the silken night.

Steel meets fire, with a crackling song,
Rhythms pulse, where they belong.
Each spark a wish, bright and bold,
Stories of courage, within them told.

As hammers clash, and anvils sing,
The air is filled with wondrous bling.
In every flicker, dreams take flight,
A magical ballet, through the night.

With every turn, and every twist,
Shadows embrace, in an artisan's mist.
They mold their visions, without restraint,
In the heart of the forge, no room for faint.

Let the sparks dance, let them fly,
In the flames, let the spirits cry.
For in this realm, where passions reside,
The dance of glistening sparks shall guide.

Threads of Light in the Weaver's Glance

With whispers soft, the weaver starts,
Threads of light, stitched with hearts.
A loom that hums, with stories deep,
In each delicate weave, secrets keep.

Yarns of color, both bright and pale,
Crafted tales that never pale.
In the tapestry's dance, life unfurls,
Threads of joy, where sorrow whirls.

With every pull, a tale is spun,
Echoes of laughter, of battles won.
The weaver's glance, both wise and keen,
Watches the story, in every scene.

As day surrenders, to twilight's gleam,
The woven path becomes a dream.
In the flickering night, their magic glows,
In threads of light, the journey flows.

So gather the threads, and spin the night,
For in the weaver's glance, all is right.
The fabric of life, in every strand,
Threads of light, by gentlest hand.

Resonance of the Amethyst Craft

In twilight's whisper, the amethyst gleams,
Crafting dreams from the moon's silver beams.
Each facet holds stories, both ancient and new,
A tapestry woven from starlit dew.

With hands that are guided by magic's soft song,
The artisans gather, where they all belong.
Their laughter like echoes of spells in the air,
Resonating secrets, beyond compare.

A dance of the crystals, in hues rich and deep,
Awakens the wonders from slumber and sleep.
In the heart of the forge, a flicker of fire,
Ignites all the passions that never expire.

From shadows emerge the most delicate shapes,
Molding enchantments, as time gently drapes.
Each strike of the hammer, a magical chime,
Ringing through realms that are lost to all time.

When twilight descends, and the craftwork is done,
The amethyst glimmers as bright as the sun.
A resonance lingers, a promise unspoken,
In the heartbeats of magic, forever unbroken.

Shimmers of a Celestial Workshop

In the heart of the cosmos, a workshop awakens,
Where stars are as jewels, no beauty forsaken.
Between silver and azure, the shimmers ignite,
Crafting wonders from whispers of the night.

The celestial artisans gather in grace,
Weaving a tapestry, time cannot erase.
With brushes of starlight, their colors appear,
Each stroke a memory, each shimmer a tear.

Glistening orbs twirl in a dance of their making,
Reflecting the joy of the cosmos' waking.
In this haven of dreams, creation takes flight,
A symphony written in the silence of night.

From nebulous clouds, they forge and they mold,
Unraveling stories, both gentle and bold.
A nebula's embrace, a comet's bright tail,
Each shimmer a heartbeat, a cosmic exhale.

As twilight approaches, the workshop will glow,
With hints of the magic that nobody knows.
In the shimmers of darkness, the stars will align,
A celestial promise, a dance so divine.

Mystical Reflections in the Alloyed Light

In the forge of the twilight, the metals entwine,
Creating reflections that shimmer and shine.
Each spark is a whisper of magic retold,
In the alloyed light, where the stories unfold.

Crafted by hands that are guided by fate,
The essence of wonder can never abate.
From copper to silver, from gold into gray,
The metals respond to the twilight's ballet.

In the crucible's embrace, a symphony plays,
Melodies echoing the ancient ways.
Each element dances, a magical sight,
As reflections unfold in the alloyed light.

Through whimsical union, they whisper with glee,
The secrets of ages, both sweet and carefree.
In the glow of the forge, a new story starts,
Merging with laughter, connecting all hearts.

With shadows as partners, and dreams as their muse,
They shape the impossible, nothing to lose.
In mystical realms where creation takes flight,
Magic resides in the alloyed light.

Twilight's Glow in the Metal Mirage

In twilight's embrace, the metals ignite,
Creating a mirage, surreal in the night.
Glistening shadows dance on the floor,
A vision of beauty, forever to adore.

Through a tapestry woven of steel and of brass,
The essence of twilight doth shimmer and pass.
Each angle reflects a world borne anew,
As the twilight draws close, with colors that woo.

Beneath the soft glow, the enchantments arise,
Forged in the heat of the sunset's disguise.
Starlit vibrations ripple through the air,
Inviting the wanderers to linger and stare.

From the depths of the forge, a spell softly calls,
Weaving its magic through shadowed halls.
As twilight unfolds, the mirage takes form,
A dreamlike illusion that dances, a storm.

With whispers of metal, where silence is spun,
The craft of creation has only begun.
In twilight's warm glow, from dusk until dawn,
The beauty of magic will always live on.

Whispers of the Celestial Forge

In shadows deep, where hammers sing,
The stars align, their secrets cling.
Crafted dreams in gilded flight,
Forge of hope, in endless night.

The anvil's call, a faint refrain,
Echoes of love, joy, and pain.
With every strike, the world anew,
A tapestry of stars, untrue.

Whispers weave through silken air,
Carried by the night's sweet care.
In molten gold, desires flow,
A dance of light in twilight's glow.

The pulse of time, a rhythmic beat,
Ancient tales and visions meet.
Craftsmen's hands, both rough and skilled,
Shape the dreams the heart has thrilled.

So listen close, when silence falls,
For in the quiet, magic calls.
In celestial fires, bright and bold,
The forge reveals what's yet untold.

Luminous Mist on the Anvil's Edge

Softly glows the morning mist,
Where secrets lie and dreams exist.
The anvil waits, with silent grace,
For hands of fate to find their place.

Each breath a spark, each heartbeat, light,
In luminous embrace of night.
Molding futures from the air,
Crafting wonders with tender care.

In swirling fog, the ancients stir,
With whispered lore and voices pure.
They guide the hammer, fulfill the wish,
With every clang, a siren's swish.

The radiant dance of dawn's first glow,
Awakens dreams that ebb and flow.
In shadows cast by light so bright,
The edges blur, day into night.

The artisan's heart is brave, yet shy,
Holding truths too deep to pry.
In mist's embrace, the world believes,
That magic grows on whispered leaves.

So linger near, where soft light glows,
And find the path that wisdom shows.
For on the anvil, hopes are spun,
With every dawn, a world begun.

Enchanted Tears of the Seraph

From heaven's height, a song descends,
In crystal drops, the heart mends.
Tears of joy, flame of the stars,
Spilling light through cosmic bars.

Each droplet tells of rivers wide,
Where dreams take wing, in hope they glide.
Sacred whispers in the night,
Guide lost souls to realms of light.

With every tear, a tale unfolds,
Of love unbound, and bravery bold.
The seraph's heart, a beacon strong,
In darkness finds where it belongs.

Beneath the veil of silver skies,
And gentle winds that softly sighs,
Ancient stories roam the air,
To touch the hearts that seek and dare.

In each embrace, the unseen spark,
Illuminates the heavens dark.
With enchanted tears, the journey starts,
To bind the realms, and heal the hearts.

So shed not tears of sorrow deep,
For beauty lies where angels weep.
In every drop, a world anew,
The blessed light will guide you through.

Twilight's Embrace in the Artisan's Workshop

In twilight's glow, the shadows dance,
With tools of craft, they weave romance.
A gentle hush, the world awaits,
As artistry unlocks the gates.

Among the shelves, old whispers sigh,
Of dreams once lived, now passing by.
The artisan smiles, with patient hands,
Creates the magic, where heart understands.

With every stroke, a vision clear,
The soul of twilight whispers near.
In fragments bright, the stars align,
Where hopes are forged and shadows shine.

The candle's light, a guiding friend,
Through corners dark where wonders blend.
The heart's true song begins to hum,
In twilight's arms, the future's come.

So linger now, let dreams take flight,
In artisan's realm, where all feels right.
For in the glow of day's last kiss,
Awaits the magic none can miss.

In twilight's embrace, the world unfolds,
A tapestry of stories told.
The artisan's touch, both kind and wise,
Sees beauty rise in soft goodbyes.

Twilight Hues in Forged Shadows

As daylight fades, the shadows loom,
Whispers of twilight, a soft-brimmed gloom.
Starfire dances on the edge of night,
Wrapped in a shroud of indigo light.

Echoes of laughter haunt ancient trees,
Stirring the secrets carried by the breeze.
In the stillness, dreams begin to weave,
A tapestry of wonders, we believe.

Crimson streaks kiss the horizon bright,
Painting the world in a delicate light.
Forged in the silence, shadows take flight,
Beneath the gaze of the emerging night.

The air is thick with forgotten tales,
Of brave hearts and ships that caught the gales.
Twilight's embrace, a caress so deep,
Cradling the magic that stirs from sleep.

In moments like these, we glimpse what's true,
In the darkness, old fears we construe.
Yet through the twilight, hope's flicker shines,
In forged shadows, fate's thread intertwines.

The Alchemy of Rebirth

In the forge of dreams where visions glow,
Brass and silver meet, a magic flow.
Through trials of fire, the essence is found,
Setting the stage for the soul's rebound.

From ashes we rise, as phoenixes soar,
In the dance of the elements, spirits implore.
With heartbeats of thunder and whispers of wind,
The alchemy of rebirth soon begins.

Eclipses of shadows, we summon the light,
Casting away darkness, embracing the fight.
Each fragment transformed, a new story told,
In this sacred circle, we brave and bold.

Mending the fractures with golden embrace,
Fate's thread rewoven in time's vast space.
A journey of wonder, a quest so grand,
Finding our strength in this enchanted land.

So gather the remnants, let magic ignite,
In the hearts of the daring, forever alight.
For within us lies power, untamed and true,
The alchemy of rebirth, waiting for you.

Glistening Wishes in the Artisan's Realm

In the artisan's realm where dreams take flight,
Wishes glisten like stars in the night.
With nimble fingers, craft visions anew,
Transforming the morning mist into dew.

Each trinket of hope, a tale to be spun,
In colors of embers, beneath the warm sun.
From silver and stone to fabric and thread,
Weaving the whispers of things left unsaid.

The dance of creation, a jubilant beat,
As laughter and passion blend in the heat.
Glistening wishes, like pollen in spring,
Blooming with promise in every small thing.

Hands stained with colors of vibrant delight,
Mosaic of journeys tastefully bright.
In the heart of the artisan, echoes resound,
Each moment a treasure in brilliance found.

So venture within this enchanted space,
Where dreams converge with a delicate grace.
In glistening wishes, our spirits ignite,
Crafting the magic that livens the night.

Moonlit Conversations with Iron Spirits

Beneath the soft glow of a silvery moon,
Iron spirits awaken, a haunting tune.
Whispers of metal, a rhythmic refrain,
Singing of wonders beyond human pain.

In shadows they linger, both brave and bold,
Tales of old battles and legends retold.
They dance in the rafters, unseen but near,
Guardians of secrets, with stories to share.

Cloaked in the night, their murmurs arise,
Echoing truths beneath starlit skies.
Wisdom in rust, in each mark and scar,
Moonlit conversations reach near and far.

What dreams may emerge when spirits confide?
In the cooling dusk, let imagination guide.
Listen closely, for magic may breathe,
In dialogue woven with hope and belief.

With each passing hour, the whispering fades,
Yet linger the echoes, in memory's shades.
In moonlit embrace, they fade from our sight,
Leaving behind glimmers of mystical light.

www.ingramcontent.com/pod-product-compliance
Ingram Content Group UK Ltd.
Pitfield, Milton Keynes, MK11 3LW, UK
UKHW021433160125
4146UKWH00006B/80